AF575869

Shukr

An Inspirational Dua and Gratitude Journal for Women

Gabrielle Deonath

In loving memory of Sister Hamida Khan,
who touched so many lives with her humanity and kindness,
who taught so many women about the beauty of Islam.

Published by:
Ulysses Press
PO Box 3440
Berkeley, CA 94703
www.ulyssespress.com

ISBN: 978-1-64604-328-6
Library of Congress Control Number: 2021946377

Printed in the United States by Versa Press
2 4 6 8 10 9 7 5 3 1

Acquisitions editor: Casie Vogel
Managing editor: Claire Chun
Editor: Michele Anderson
Proofreader: Renee Rutledge
Front cover design: Hafsa Khan
Interior design: Raquel Castro
Production assistant: Yesenia Garcia-Lopez

Contents

Introduction

Dear ________________________,
(your name here)

This journal was created especially with you—the modern Muslim woman—in mind. While a number of gratitude journals or prayer journals are available for women of other faiths, few of those books directly cater to the Muslimah.

As women, we are often overwhelmed with responsibilities and obligations in various areas of our lives, especially in our careers and personal relationships. I feel those pressures in my own life, even as a single woman in my mid-twenties. While I don't have a house to run or children to take care of, I still feel like there aren't enough hours in the day to take care of myself in all the ways I know I should—physically, mentally, emotionally, and spiritually. When I have to pick and choose how to practice self-care, I have often pushed my faith to the bottom of the to-do list. The more women I speak to, the more I realize how common this problem is for many of us, across all adult age groups.

Shukr aims to help you prioritize your relationship with Allah (SWT) by giving you space to reflect on hadiths, duas, and ayahs from the Qur'an in small bites that fit into your busy schedule. This journal is broken up into six sections centered on topics relevant to our daily lives.

Belief & Worship will push you to think about what it means to have faith as a Muslim and how you can continue to grow your relationship with Allah (SWT).

Relationships will focus on the other important bonds in your life—especially those with your parents, siblings, children, and spouse.

Growth & Success will encourage you to reflect on personal and professional development, as well as on how you define success in this life.

Health will explore Islam's view on physical and mental health, as well as Islam's view on emotional well-being.

Community will help you to remember that you are part of something much larger than yourself—the Muslim Ummah. This section will allow you to discover the importance of keeping your communities in your heart and mind.

While each of these five sections will provide you with selections of well-known duas, hadiths, and verses from the Qur'an, the prompts will remain consistent to help you develop the habit of analyzing Islamic texts in a deep, meaningful way. Each entry is allotted two pages: The first page will focus on your interpretation of the selection and how you can incorporate what you learned into your daily life; the second will be centered on expressing your gratitude to Allah (SWT) and exploring your spiritual needs to help build a foundation for your duas. At the end of each section will be three blank entries that you can use to reflect on the selections of your choice.

In the final section, **Reflections**, you will find prompts that encourage you to reflect on your spiritual journey over the course of completing this journal. It was important for me to give space to these prompts because the purpose of this journal is not only for you to learn more about our beautiful religion but

also to gain a deeper understanding of ourselves as individuals, as women, as Muslimahs.

My personal relationship with Islam and Allah is ever evolving. It has ebbed and flowed in different phases of my life, but I am grateful that something always pulls me back to Allah (SWT), reaffirms my iman, and continues to keep faith at the center of my life.

When I was a child, I gained a basic understanding of the tenets of Islam as a student at an Islamic elementary school. As I moved into public school, I continued my studies with private Qur'an lessons. In high school, I started attending a women's halaqa at my local masjid. In gaining more knowledge about Islam there, I made the decision to begin wearing hijab at age fifteen. I strongly believe that because of that choice, Allah led me to my career as a writer. I found my voice and my "occasion for writing," as we writers say. I became a published writer at age sixteen, penning personal essays about my experience as a Muslim American teenager. And then in college, I found my place as president of the Muslim Students Association for two years.

Now fully out of school and having entered into full-fledged adulthood, I know that it's up to me to find ways to continue my spiritual growth. It's not as easy when a teacher or a parent is no longer watching over you, yet still I see the miraculous ways in which I am reminded of the importance of my relationship with Allah (SWT). I came across the opportunity to create this journal at the most unexpected, yet perfect, time, and the process of putting this book together has continued to help my relationship with Allah (SWT) and my knowledge of and love for Islam to flourish.

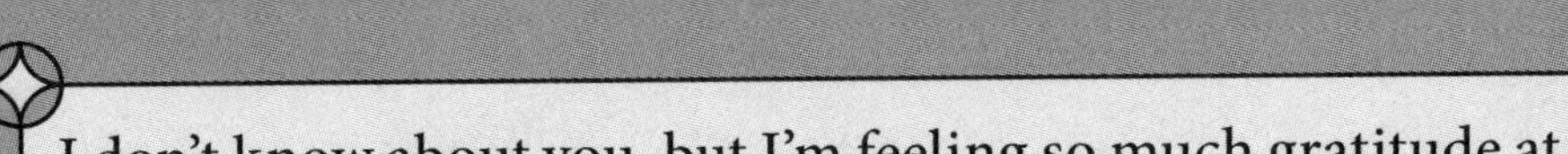

I don't know about you, but I'm feeling so much gratitude at this moment. I hope reading a little bit of my story inspires you to reflect on the divine ways in which Allah (SWT) has pulled you close to Him in your life, and I hope it inspires you to feel shukr in the depths of your heart as you begin this journal. If you take away anything from this journaling experience, I hope it is this: When you seek Allah (SWT), He will be there.

Allah (SWT) said:
"Whoever comes towards Me, I rush towards him."

[Sahih Muslim]

With love and gratitude,
Gabrielle Deonath

Note: All Qur'anic translations have been taken from Dr. Mustafa Khattab's *The Clear Quran*. The authenticity of all hadiths has been verified by Shaykh Ibad Wali. The hadiths included in this journal are graded as Sahih or Hasan.

8 Tips for Making Dua

When you make dua, it is your one-on-one time with Allah (SWT) to ask for whatever you wish and to speak from your heart. To increase the chances of your prayers being accepted, here are eight tips to keep in mind:

- **Say your duas out loud.**
  Do not recite your prayers too loudly or silently but seek a way between. *[Qur'an, 17:110]*
- **Begin by praising Allah (SWT).**
  Amr bin Malik Al-Janbi narrated that he heard Fadalah bin `Ubaid saying: "The Prophet (SAW) said: 'When one of you performs Salat, then let him begin by expressing gratitude to Allah and praising Him...'" *[Jami at-Tirmidhi]*
- **Send prayers upon the Prophet (SAW).**
  "...Then, let him send Salat upon the Prophet (SAW), then let him supplicate after that, whatever he wishes." *[Jami at-Tirmidhi]*
- **Mention the attributes of Allah (SWT) using the ninety-nine names in a way that relates to your duas.**
  Allah has the Most Beautiful Names. So call upon Him by them." *[Qu'ran, 7:180]*
- **Ask for forgiveness.**
  On the authority of Anas (RA), who said:
  I heard the Messenger of Allah (SAW) say: "Allah the Almighty said: 'O son of Adam, so long as you call upon Me and ask of Me, I shall forgive you for what you have done, and I shall not mind. O son of Adam, were your sins to reach the clouds of the sky and were

you then to ask forgiveness of Me, I would forgive you. O son of Adam, were you to come to Me with sins nearly as great as the earth and were you then to face Me, ascribing no partner to Me, I would bring you forgiveness nearly as great as it.'" *[40 Hadith Qudsi]*

- **Mention good deeds you have done for the sake of Allah (SWT).**
  `Abdullah bin `Umar narrated:
  The Prophet (SAW) said, "While three men were walking, it started raining and they took shelter in a cave in a mountain. A big rock rolled down from the mountain and closed the mouth of the cave. They said to each other, 'Think of good deeds which you did for Allah's sake only and invoke Allah by giving reference to those deeds so that He may remove this rock from you.'" *[Sahih al-Bukhari]*

- **Make dua for others.**
  Abu Dharr reported that Allah's Messenger (SAW) said: "There is no believing servant who supplicates for his brother behind his back (in his absence) that the Angels do not say: 'The same be for you too.'" *[Sahih Muslim]*

- **Make dua often and not just in times of need.**
  Abu Hurairah (RA) narrated:
  The Messenger of Allah (SAW) said: "Whoever wishes that Allah would respond to him during hardship and grief, then let him supplicate plentifully when at ease." *[Jami at-Tirmidhi]*

The Best Times to Make Dua

There is never a wrong time to speak to Allah (SWT) and ask Him for whatever you may need. However, there are certain times when a Muslim is considered to be closest to Allah (SWT) and it is more likely for their duas to be accepted. According to authentic hadiths, these are some of the best times to make dua.

- **In the last third of the night**
  Abu Hurairah (RA) narrated:
  Allah's Messenger (SAW) said, "Our Lord, the Blessed, the Superior, comes every night down on the nearest Heaven to us when the last third of the night remains, saying: 'Is there anyone to invoke Me, so that I may respond to invocation? Is there anyone to ask Me, so that I may grant him his request? Is there anyone seeking My forgiveness, so that I may forgive him?'" *[Sahih al-Bukhari]*
- **Between the Adhan and Iqamah**
  Anas bin Malik narrated:
  Allah's Messenger (SAW) said, "The supplication made between the Adhan and Iqamah is not rejected." *[Jami at-Tirmidhi]*
- **Before breaking your fast**
  Abu Hurairah (RA) narrated that the Messenger of Allah (SAW) said:
  "There are three whose supplication is not rejected: The fasting person when he breaks his fast, the just leader, and the supplication of the oppressed person; Allah raises it up above the clouds and opens the gates of heaven to it. And the Lord says: 'By My might, I shall surely aid you, even if it should be after a while.'" *[Jami at-Tirmidhi]*

- **An hour on Friday**
  Abu Hurairah (RA) narrated:
  Allah's Messenger (SAW) talked about Friday and said, "There is an hour on Friday[1] and if a Muslim gets it while offering Salat and asks something from Allah (SWT), then Allah (SWT) will definitely meet his demand." And he (the Prophet [SAW]) pointed out the shortness of that particular time with his hands. *[Sahih al-Bukhari]*
- **In sujood**
  Abu Hurairah (RA) reported:
  The Messenger of Allah (SAW) said, "The nearest a servant comes to his Lord is when he is prostrating himself, so make supplication (in this state)." *[Sahih Muslim]*
- **After obligatory prayers**
  Abu Umamah narrated:
  It was said, "O Messenger of Allah, which supplication is most likely to be listened to?" He said: "(During) the last part of the night and at the end of the obligatory prayers." *[Jami at-Tirmidhi]*
- **While traveling**
  Abu Hurairah (RA) narrated:
  The Messenger of Allah (SAW) said, "Three supplications are accepted, there is no doubt in them (about them being accepted): The supplication of the oppressed, the supplication of the traveler, and the supplication of his father against his son." *[Jami at-Tirmidhi]*

1 There are two opinions on what this hour is. Some scholars say it is from after `Asr until the sun sets. Other scholars say it is from the time the imam sits on the pulpit for khutbah until the end of the jumu'ah prayer.

- **On Laylat-ul-Qadr**
  A'isha (RA) narrated that she said:
  "O Messenger of Allah, what do you think I should say in my supplication, if I come upon Laylat-ul-Qadr?"
  He said: "Say 'Allahumma innaka 'afuwwun tuhibbul-'afwa, fa'fu 'anni [O Allah, You are Forgiving and love forgiveness, so forgive me].'" *[Ibn Majah]*

- **The Day of Arafat**
  A'isha (RA) reported that Allah's Messenger (SAW) said: "There is no day when God sets free more servants from Hell than the Day of Arafat. He draws near, then praises them to the angels, saying: 'What do these servants want?'" *[Sahih Muslim]*

Belief

&

Worship

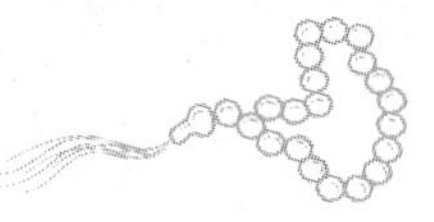

Do people think once they say, "We believe," that they will be left without being put to the test?

[Qur'an, 29:2]

WHAT DOES THIS AYAH MEAN TO YOU?

HOW DOES THIS RELATE TO YOUR DAILY LIFE?

WHAT ARE THREE THINGS THAT YOU CAN EXPRESS SHUKR FOR IN YOUR DUA TODAY? WHY ARE YOU GRATEFUL FOR THEM?

WHAT IS ONE THING THAT YOU WOULD LIKE TO ASK FOR IN YOUR DUA TODAY? HOW WOULD IT HELP YOU IF ALLAH GRANTED IT TO YOU?

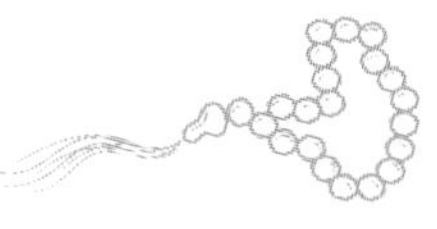

Anas (RA) narrated:

The Prophet (SAW) said, "None of you will have faith till he wishes for his (Muslim) brother what he likes for himself."

[Sahih al-Bukhari]

WHAT DOES THIS HADITH MEAN TO YOU?

HOW DOES THIS RELATE TO YOUR DAILY LIFE?

WHAT ARE THREE THINGS THAT YOU CAN EXPRESS SHUKR FOR IN YOUR DUA TODAY? WHY ARE YOU GRATEFUL FOR THEM?

WHAT IS ONE THING THAT YOU WOULD LIKE TO ASK FOR IN YOUR DUA TODAY? HOW WOULD IT HELP YOU IF ALLAH GRANTED IT TO YOU?

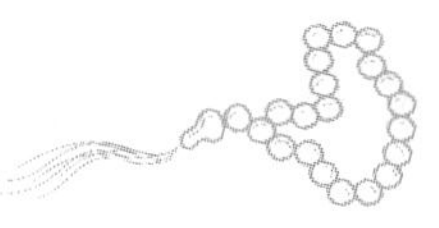

Abu Hurairah (RA) narrated:

Allah's Messenger (SAW) said, "By Him in Whose Hands my life is, none of you will have faith till he loves me more than his father and his children."

[Sahih al-Bukhari]

WHAT DOES THIS HADITH MEAN TO YOU?

HOW DOES THIS RELATE TO YOUR DAILY LIFE?

WHAT ARE THREE THINGS THAT YOU CAN EXPRESS SHUKR FOR IN YOUR DUA TODAY? WHY ARE YOU GRATEFUL FOR THEM?

WHAT IS ONE THING THAT YOU WOULD LIKE TO ASK FOR IN YOUR DUA TODAY? HOW WOULD IT HELP YOU IF ALLAH GRANTED IT TO YOU?

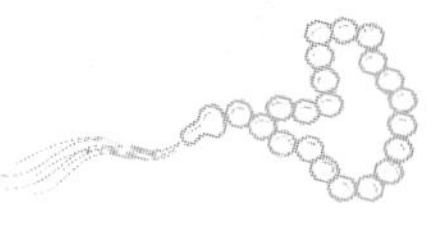

Abu Said Al-Khudri narrated:

The Prophet (SAW) said, "When the people of Paradise will enter Paradise and the people of Hell will go to Hell, Allah will order those who have had faith equal to the weight of a grain of mustard seed to be taken out from Hell."

[Sahih al-Bukhari]

WHAT DOES THIS HADITH MEAN TO YOU?

HOW DOES THIS RELATE TO YOUR DAILY LIFE?

WHAT ARE THREE THINGS THAT YOU CAN EXPRESS SHUKR FOR IN YOUR DUA TODAY? WHY ARE YOU GRATEFUL FOR THEM?

WHAT IS ONE THING THAT YOU WOULD LIKE TO ASK FOR IN YOUR DUA TODAY? HOW WOULD IT HELP YOU IF ALLAH GRANTED IT TO YOU?

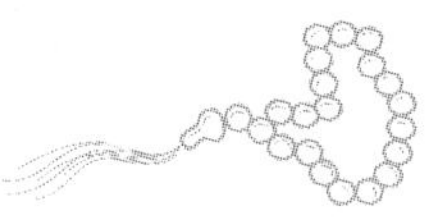

Abu Hurairah (RA) narrated:

The Prophet (SAW) said, "Religion is very easy and whoever overburdens himself in his religion will not be able to continue in that way. So you should not be extremists but try to be near to perfection and receive the good tidings that you will be rewarded; and gain strength by worshipping in the mornings, the afternoons, and during the last hours of the nights."

[Sahih al-Bukhari]

WHAT DOES THIS HADITH MEAN TO YOU?

HOW DOES THIS RELATE TO YOUR DAILY LIFE?

WHAT ARE THREE THINGS THAT YOU CAN EXPRESS SHUKR FOR IN YOUR DUA TODAY? WHY ARE YOU GRATEFUL FOR THEM?

WHAT IS ONE THING THAT YOU WOULD LIKE TO ASK FOR IN YOUR DUA TODAY? HOW WOULD IT HELP YOU IF ALLAH GRANTED IT TO YOU?

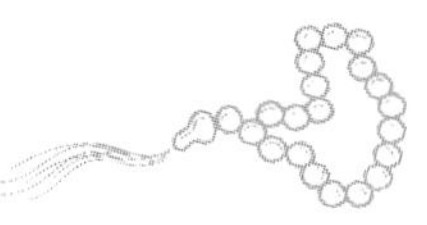

Our Lord! Do not let our hearts deviate after you have guided us. Grant us Your mercy. You are indeed the Giver of all bounties.

[Qur'an, 3:8]

WHAT DOES THIS DUA MEAN TO YOU?

HOW DOES THIS RELATE TO YOUR DAILY LIFE?

WHAT ARE THREE THINGS THAT YOU CAN EXPRESS SHUKR FOR IN YOUR DUA TODAY? WHY ARE YOU GRATEFUL FOR THEM?

WHAT IS ONE THING THAT YOU WOULD LIKE TO ASK FOR IN YOUR DUA TODAY? HOW WOULD IT HELP YOU IF ALLAH GRANTED IT TO YOU?

This is the Book! There is no doubt about it—a guide for those mindful of God, who believe in the unseen, establish prayer, and donate from what We have provided for them, and who believe in what has been revealed to you O Prophet and what was revealed before you, and have sure faith in the Hereafter. It is they who are truly guided by their Lord, and it is they who will be successful.

[Qur'an, 2:2–5]

WHAT DO THESE AYAHS MEAN TO YOU?

HOW DOES THIS RELATE TO YOUR DAILY LIFE?

WHAT ARE THREE THINGS THAT YOU CAN EXPRESS SHUKR FOR IN YOUR DUA TODAY? WHY ARE YOU GRATEFUL FOR THEM?

WHAT IS ONE THING THAT YOU WOULD LIKE TO ASK FOR IN YOUR DUA TODAY? HOW WOULD IT HELP YOU IF ALLAH GRANTED IT TO YOU?

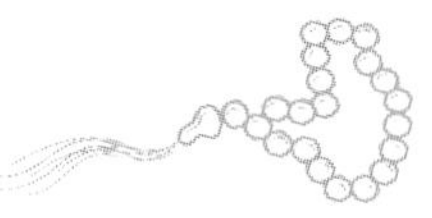

No calamity befalls anyone except by God's Will. And whoever has faith in God, He will rightly guide their hearts through adversity.... God—there is no god worthy of worship except Him. So in God let the believers put their trust.

[Qur'an, 64:11–13]

WHAT DO THESE AYAHS MEAN TO YOU?

HOW DOES THIS RELATE TO YOUR DAILY LIFE?

WHAT ARE THREE THINGS THAT YOU CAN EXPRESS SHUKR FOR IN YOUR DUA TODAY? WHY ARE YOU GRATEFUL FOR THEM?

WHAT IS ONE THING THAT YOU WOULD LIKE TO ASK FOR IN YOUR DUA TODAY? HOW WOULD IT HELP YOU IF ALLAH GRANTED IT TO YOU?

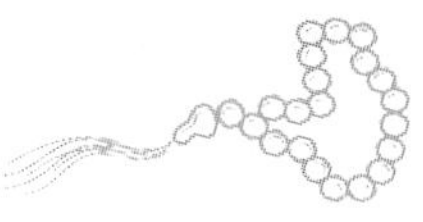

WRITE YOUR DUA, HADITH, OR QUR'AN SELECTION HERE:

WHAT DOES THIS SELECTION MEAN TO YOU?

HOW DOES THIS RELATE TO YOUR DAILY LIFE?

WHAT ARE THREE THINGS THAT YOU CAN EXPRESS SHUKR FOR IN YOUR DUA TODAY? WHY ARE YOU GRATEFUL FOR THEM?

WHAT IS ONE THING THAT YOU WOULD LIKE TO ASK FOR IN YOUR DUA TODAY? HOW WOULD IT HELP YOU IF ALLAH GRANTED IT TO YOU?

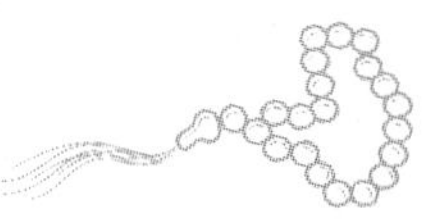

WRITE YOUR DUA, HADITH, OR QUR'AN SELECTION HERE:

WHAT DOES THIS SELECTION MEAN TO YOU?

HOW DOES THIS RELATE TO YOUR DAILY LIFE?

WHAT ARE THREE THINGS THAT YOU CAN EXPRESS SHUKR FOR IN YOUR DUA TODAY? WHY ARE YOU GRATEFUL FOR THEM?

WHAT IS ONE THING THAT YOU WOULD LIKE TO ASK FOR IN YOUR DUA TODAY? HOW WOULD IT HELP YOU IF ALLAH GRANTED IT TO YOU?

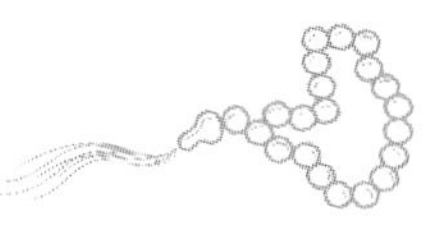

WRITE YOUR DUA, HADITH, OR QUR'AN SELECTION HERE:

WHAT DOES THIS SELECTION MEAN TO YOU?

HOW DOES THIS RELATE TO YOUR DAILY LIFE?

WHAT ARE THREE THINGS THAT YOU CAN EXPRESS SHUKR FOR IN YOUR DUA TODAY? WHY ARE YOU GRATEFUL FOR THEM?

WHAT IS ONE THING THAT YOU WOULD LIKE TO ASK FOR IN YOUR DUA TODAY? HOW WOULD IT HELP YOU IF ALLAH GRANTED IT TO YOU?

Relationships

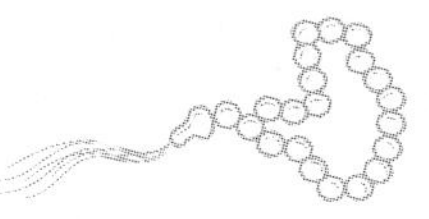

For your Lord has decreed that you worship none but Him. And honor your parents. If one or both of them reach old age in your care, never say to them even "ugh," nor yell at them. Rather, address them respectfully. And be humble with them out of mercy, and pray, "My Lord! Be merciful to them as they raised me when I was young."

[Qur'an, 17:23–24]

WHAT DO THESE AYAHS MEAN TO YOU?

HOW DOES THIS RELATE TO YOUR DAILY LIFE?

WHAT ARE THREE THINGS THAT YOU CAN EXPRESS SHUKR FOR IN YOUR DUA TODAY? WHY ARE YOU GRATEFUL FOR THEM?

WHAT IS ONE THING THAT YOU WOULD LIKE TO ASK FOR IN YOUR DUA TODAY? HOW WOULD IT HELP YOU IF ALLAH GRANTED IT TO YOU?

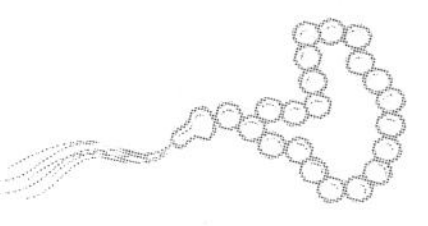

Abu Hurairah (RA) reported:

A person said, "Allah's Messenger, who amongst the people is most deserving of my good treatment?" He said, "Your mother, again your mother, again your mother, then your father, then your nearest relatives according to the order (of nearness)."

[Sahih Muslim]

WHAT DOES THIS HADITH MEAN TO YOU?

HOW DOES THIS RELATE TO YOUR DAILY LIFE?

WHAT ARE THREE THINGS THAT YOU CAN EXPRESS SHUKR FOR IN YOUR DUA TODAY? WHY ARE YOU GRATEFUL FOR THEM?

WHAT IS ONE THING THAT YOU WOULD LIKE TO ASK FOR IN YOUR DUA TODAY? HOW WOULD IT HELP YOU IF ALLAH GRANTED IT TO YOU?

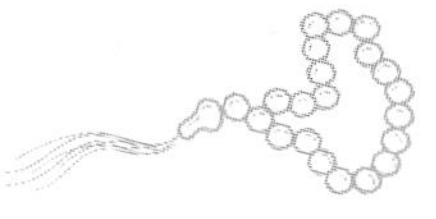

`Abdullah bin `Amr narrated:

The Prophet (SAW) said, "Al-Wasil (the one who maintains ties of kinship) is not the one who recompenses the good done to him by his relatives, but Al-Wasil is the one who keeps good relations with those relatives who had severed the bond of kinship with him."

[Sahih al-Bukhari]

WHAT DOES THIS HADITH MEAN TO YOU?

HOW DOES THIS RELATE TO YOUR DAILY LIFE?

WHAT ARE THREE THINGS THAT YOU CAN EXPRESS SHUKR FOR IN YOUR DUA TODAY? WHY ARE YOU GRATEFUL FOR THEM?

WHAT IS ONE THING THAT YOU WOULD LIKE TO ASK FOR IN YOUR DUA TODAY? HOW WOULD IT HELP YOU IF ALLAH GRANTED IT TO YOU?

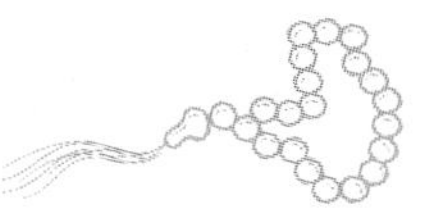

And one of His signs is that He created for you spouses from among yourselves so that you may find comfort in them. And He has placed between you compassion and mercy. Surely in this are signs for people who reflect.

[Qur'an, 30:21]

WHAT DOES THIS AYAH MEAN TO YOU?

HOW DOES THIS RELATE TO YOUR DAILY LIFE?

WHAT ARE THREE THINGS THAT YOU CAN EXPRESS SHUKR FOR IN YOUR DUA TODAY? WHY ARE YOU GRATEFUL FOR THEM?

WHAT IS ONE THING THAT YOU WOULD LIKE TO ASK FOR IN YOUR DUA TODAY? HOW WOULD IT HELP YOU IF ALLAH GRANTED IT TO YOU?

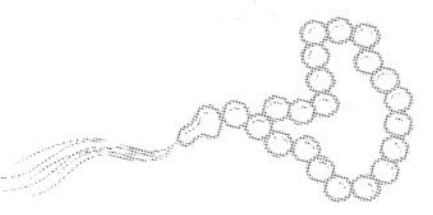

They [the true servants of the Most Compassionate] are those who pray, "Our Lord! Bless us with pious spouses and offspring who will be the joy of hearts and make us models for the righteous."

[Qur'an, 25:74]

WHAT DOES THIS DUA MEAN TO YOU?

HOW DOES THIS RELATE TO YOUR DAILY LIFE?

WHAT ARE THREE THINGS THAT YOU CAN EXPRESS SHUKR FOR IN YOUR DUA TODAY? WHY ARE YOU GRATEFUL FOR THEM?

WHAT IS ONE THING THAT YOU WOULD LIKE TO ASK FOR IN YOUR DUA TODAY? HOW WOULD IT HELP YOU IF ALLAH GRANTED IT TO YOU?

I seek protection for you in the Perfect Words of Allah from every devil and every beast, and from every envious blameworthy eye.

[Bukhari]

WHAT DOES THIS DUA MEAN TO YOU?

HOW DOES THIS RELATE TO YOUR DAILY LIFE?

WHAT ARE THREE THINGS THAT YOU CAN EXPRESS SHUKR FOR IN YOUR DUA TODAY? WHY ARE YOU GRATEFUL FOR THEM?

WHAT IS ONE THING THAT YOU WOULD LIKE TO ASK FOR IN YOUR DUA TODAY? HOW WOULD IT HELP YOU IF ALLAH GRANTED IT TO YOU?

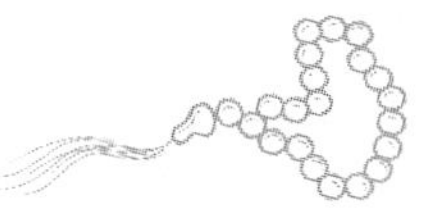

We have commanded people to honor their parents. Their mothers bore them in hardship and delivered them in hardship. Their period of bearing and weaning is thirty months. In time, when the child reaches their prime at the age of forty, they pray, "My Lord! Inspire me to always be thankful for Your favors which You blessed me and my parents with, and to do good deeds that please You. And instill righteousness in my offspring. I truly repent to You, and I truly submit to Your Will."

[Qur'an, 46:15]

WHAT DOES THIS AYAH MEAN TO YOU?

HOW DOES THIS RELATE TO YOUR DAILY LIFE?

WHAT ARE THREE THINGS THAT YOU CAN EXPRESS SHUKR FOR IN YOUR DUA TODAY? WHY ARE YOU GRATEFUL FOR THEM?

WHAT IS ONE THING THAT YOU WOULD LIKE TO ASK FOR IN YOUR DUA TODAY? HOW WOULD IT HELP YOU IF ALLAH GRANTED IT TO YOU?

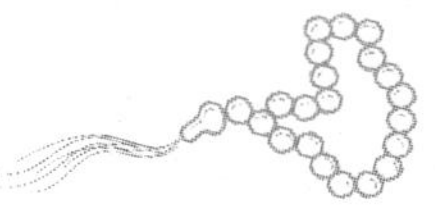

A'isha (RA) narrated:

The Messenger of Allah (SAW) said:
"The best of you is the best to his wives."

[Jami at-Tirmidhi]

WHAT DOES THIS HADITH MEAN TO YOU?

HOW DOES THIS RELATE TO YOUR DAILY LIFE?

WHAT ARE THREE THINGS THAT YOU CAN EXPRESS SHUKR FOR IN YOUR DUA TODAY? WHY ARE YOU GRATEFUL FOR THEM?

WHAT IS ONE THING THAT YOU WOULD LIKE TO ASK FOR IN YOUR DUA TODAY? HOW WOULD IT HELP YOU IF ALLAH GRANTED IT TO YOU?

Abu Ayyub Ansari reported Allah's Messenger (SAW) as saying:

"It is not permissible for a Muslim to have estranged relations with his brother [fellow Muslim] beyond three nights, the one turning one way and the other turning the other way when they meet; the better of the two is one who is the first to give a greeting."

[Sahih Muslim]

WHAT DOES THIS HADITH MEAN TO YOU?

HOW DOES THIS RELATE TO YOUR DAILY LIFE?

WHAT ARE THREE THINGS THAT YOU CAN EXPRESS SHUKR FOR IN YOUR DUA TODAY? WHY ARE YOU GRATEFUL FOR THEM?

WHAT IS ONE THING THAT YOU WOULD LIKE TO ASK FOR IN YOUR DUA TODAY? HOW WOULD IT HELP YOU IF ALLAH GRANTED IT TO YOU?

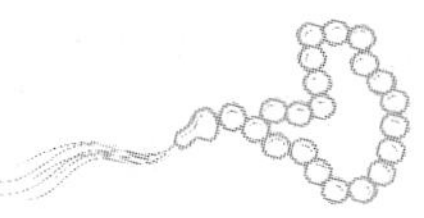

WRITE YOUR DUA, HADITH, OR QUR'AN SELECTION HERE:

WHAT DOES THIS SELECTION MEAN TO YOU?

HOW DOES THIS RELATE TO YOUR DAILY LIFE?

WHAT ARE THREE THINGS THAT YOU CAN EXPRESS SHUKR FOR IN YOUR DUA TODAY? WHY ARE YOU GRATEFUL FOR THEM?

WHAT IS ONE THING THAT YOU WOULD LIKE TO ASK FOR IN YOUR DUA TODAY? HOW WOULD IT HELP YOU IF ALLAH GRANTED IT TO YOU?

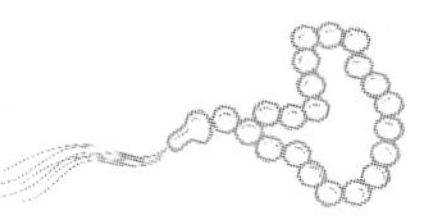

WRITE YOUR DUA, HADITH, OR QUR'AN SELECTION HERE:

WHAT DOES THIS SELECTION MEAN TO YOU?

HOW DOES THIS RELATE TO YOUR DAILY LIFE?

WHAT ARE THREE THINGS THAT YOU CAN EXPRESS SHUKR FOR IN YOUR DUA TODAY? WHY ARE YOU GRATEFUL FOR THEM?

WHAT IS ONE THING THAT YOU WOULD LIKE TO ASK FOR IN YOUR DUA TODAY? HOW WOULD IT HELP YOU IF ALLAH GRANTED IT TO YOU?

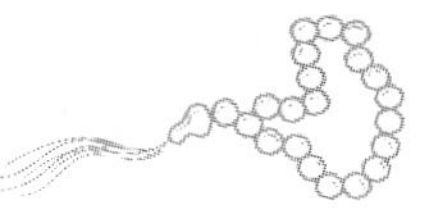

WRITE YOUR DUA, HADITH, OR QUR'AN SELECTION HERE:

WHAT DOES THIS SELECTION MEAN TO YOU?

HOW DOES THIS RELATE TO YOUR DAILY LIFE?

WHAT ARE THREE THINGS THAT YOU CAN EXPRESS SHUKR FOR IN YOUR DUA TODAY? WHY ARE YOU GRATEFUL FOR THEM?

WHAT IS ONE THING THAT YOU WOULD LIKE TO ASK FOR IN YOUR DUA TODAY? HOW WOULD IT HELP YOU IF ALLAH GRANTED IT TO YOU?

Growth

&

Success

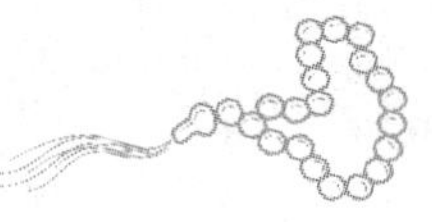

Successful indeed is the one who purifies their soul, and doomed is one who corrupts it!

[Qur'an, 91:9–10]

WHAT DO THESE AYAHS MEAN TO YOU?

HOW DOES THIS RELATE TO YOUR DAILY LIFE?

WHAT ARE THREE THINGS THAT YOU CAN EXPRESS SHUKR FOR IN YOUR DUA TODAY? WHY ARE YOU GRATEFUL FOR THEM?

WHAT IS ONE THING THAT YOU WOULD LIKE TO ASK FOR IN YOUR DUA TODAY? HOW WOULD IT HELP YOU IF ALLAH GRANTED IT TO YOU?

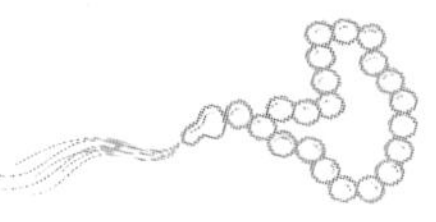

Abu Hurairah (RA) reported:

The Messenger of Allah (SAW) said, "I was sent to perfect good character."

[Al-Adab Al-Mufrad]

WHAT DOES THIS HADITH MEAN TO YOU?

HOW DOES THIS RELATE TO YOUR DAILY LIFE?

WHAT ARE THREE THINGS THAT YOU CAN EXPRESS SHUKR FOR IN YOUR DUA TODAY? WHY ARE YOU GRATEFUL FOR THEM?

WHAT IS ONE THING THAT YOU WOULD LIKE TO ASK FOR IN YOUR DUA TODAY? HOW WOULD IT HELP YOU IF ALLAH GRANTED IT TO YOU?

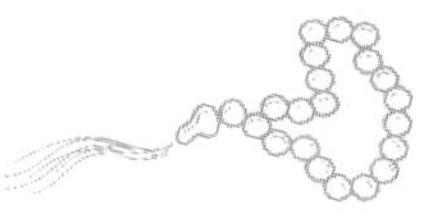

God will elevate those of you who are faithful and raise those gifted with knowledge in rank.

[Qur'an, 58:11]

WHAT DOES THIS AYAH MEAN TO YOU?

HOW DOES THIS RELATE TO YOUR DAILY LIFE?

WHAT ARE THREE THINGS THAT YOU CAN EXPRESS SHUKR FOR IN YOUR DUA TODAY? WHY ARE YOU GRATEFUL FOR THEM?

WHAT IS ONE THING THAT YOU WOULD LIKE TO ASK FOR IN YOUR DUA TODAY? HOW WOULD IT HELP YOU IF ALLAH GRANTED IT TO YOU?

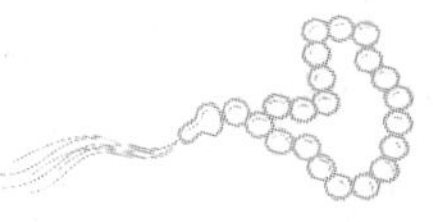

Abu Hurairah (RA) narrated: The Prophet (SAW) said, "Wealth is not in having many possessions, but rather (true) wealth is feeling sufficiency in the soul."

[Sahih al-Bukhari]

WHAT DOES THIS HADITH MEAN TO YOU?

HOW DOES THIS RELATE TO YOUR DAILY LIFE?

WHAT ARE THREE THINGS THAT YOU CAN EXPRESS SHUKR FOR IN YOUR DUA TODAY? WHY ARE YOU GRATEFUL FOR THEM?

WHAT IS ONE THING THAT YOU WOULD LIKE TO ASK FOR IN YOUR DUA TODAY? HOW WOULD IT HELP YOU IF ALLAH GRANTED IT TO YOU?

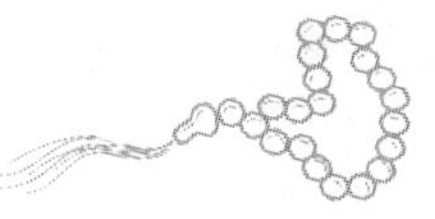

Each person will only have what they endeavored toward.

[Qur'an, 53:39]

WHAT DOES THIS AYAH MEAN TO YOU?

HOW DOES THIS RELATE TO YOUR DAILY LIFE?

WHAT ARE THREE THINGS THAT YOU CAN EXPRESS SHUKR FOR IN YOUR DUA TODAY? WHY ARE YOU GRATEFUL FOR THEM?

WHAT IS ONE THING THAT YOU WOULD LIKE TO ASK FOR IN YOUR DUA TODAY? HOW WOULD IT HELP YOU IF ALLAH GRANTED IT TO YOU?

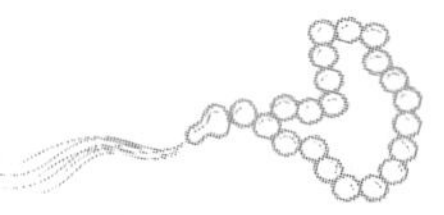

God would never change a people's state
... until they change their own state.

[Qur'an, 13:11]

WHAT DOES THIS AYAH MEAN TO YOU?

HOW DOES THIS RELATE TO YOUR DAILY LIFE?

WHAT ARE THREE THINGS THAT YOU CAN EXPRESS SHUKR FOR IN YOUR DUA TODAY? WHY ARE YOU GRATEFUL FOR THEM?

WHAT IS ONE THING THAT YOU WOULD LIKE TO ASK FOR IN YOUR DUA TODAY? HOW WOULD IT HELP YOU IF ALLAH GRANTED IT TO YOU?

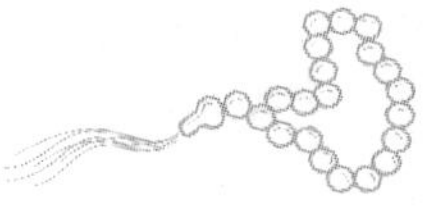

"My Lord! Uplift my heart for me, and make my task easy, and remove the impediment from my tongue so people may understand my speech."

[Qur'an, 20:25–28]

WHAT DOES THIS DUA MEAN TO YOU?

HOW DOES THIS RELATE TO YOUR DAILY LIFE?

WHAT ARE THREE THINGS THAT YOU CAN EXPRESS SHUKR FOR IN YOUR DUA TODAY? WHY ARE YOU GRATEFUL FOR THEM?

WHAT IS ONE THING THAT YOU WOULD LIKE TO ASK FOR IN YOUR DUA TODAY? HOW WOULD IT HELP YOU IF ALLAH GRANTED IT TO YOU?

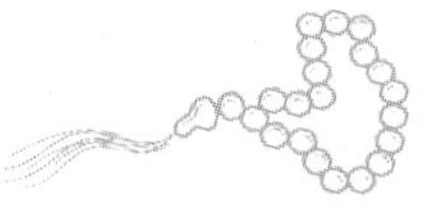

Do not rush to recite a revelation of the Qur'an O Prophet before it is properly conveyed to you, and pray, "My Lord! Increase me in knowledge."

[Qur'an, 20:114]

WHAT DOES THIS AYAH MEAN TO YOU?

HOW DOES THIS RELATE TO YOUR DAILY LIFE?

WHAT ARE THREE THINGS THAT YOU CAN EXPRESS SHUKR FOR IN YOUR DUA TODAY? WHY ARE YOU GRATEFUL FOR THEM?

WHAT IS ONE THING THAT YOU WOULD LIKE TO ASK FOR IN YOUR DUA TODAY? HOW WOULD IT HELP YOU IF ALLAH GRANTED IT TO YOU?

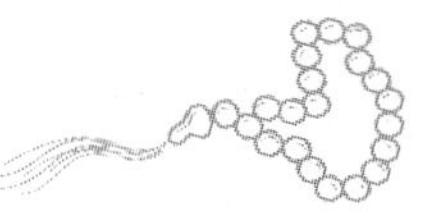

"My Lord! Grant me an honorable entrance and an honorable exit and give me a supporting authority from Yourself."

[Qur'an, 17:80]

WHAT DOES THIS DUA MEAN TO YOU?

HOW DOES THIS RELATE TO YOUR DAILY LIFE?

WHAT ARE THREE THINGS THAT YOU CAN EXPRESS SHUKR FOR IN YOUR DUA TODAY? WHY ARE YOU GRATEFUL FOR THEM?

WHAT IS ONE THING THAT YOU WOULD LIKE TO ASK FOR IN YOUR DUA TODAY? HOW WOULD IT HELP YOU IF ALLAH GRANTED IT TO YOU?

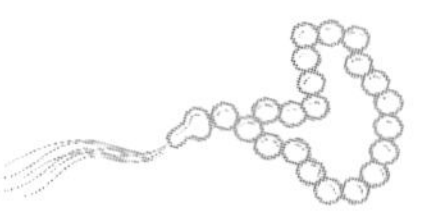

'Amr b. al–'As reported Allah's Messenger (SAW) as saying: "He is successful who has accepted Islam, who has been provided with sufficient for his want and been made contented by Allah with what He has given him."

[Sahih Muslim]

WHAT DOES THIS HADITH MEAN TO YOU?

HOW DOES THIS RELATE TO YOUR DAILY LIFE?

WHAT ARE THREE THINGS THAT YOU CAN EXPRESS SHUKR FOR IN YOUR DUA TODAY? WHY ARE YOU GRATEFUL FOR THEM?

WHAT IS ONE THING THAT YOU WOULD LIKE TO ASK FOR IN YOUR DUA TODAY? HOW WOULD IT HELP YOU IF ALLAH GRANTED IT TO YOU?

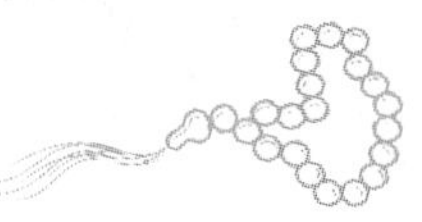

WRITE YOUR DUA, HADITH, OR QUR'AN SELECTION HERE:

WHAT DOES THIS SELECTION MEAN TO YOU?

HOW DOES THIS RELATE TO YOUR DAILY LIFE?

WHAT ARE THREE THINGS THAT YOU CAN EXPRESS SHUKR FOR IN YOUR DUA TODAY? WHY ARE YOU GRATEFUL FOR THEM?

WHAT IS ONE THING THAT YOU WOULD LIKE TO ASK FOR IN YOUR DUA TODAY? HOW WOULD IT HELP YOU IF ALLAH GRANTED IT TO YOU?

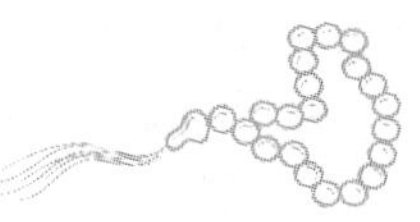

WRITE YOUR DUA, HADITH, OR QUR'AN SELECTION HERE:

WHAT DOES THIS SELECTION MEAN TO YOU?

HOW DOES THIS RELATE TO YOUR DAILY LIFE?

WHAT ARE THREE THINGS THAT YOU CAN EXPRESS SHUKR FOR IN YOUR DUA TODAY? WHY ARE YOU GRATEFUL FOR THEM?

WHAT IS ONE THING THAT YOU WOULD LIKE TO ASK FOR IN YOUR DUA TODAY? HOW WOULD IT HELP YOU IF ALLAH GRANTED IT TO YOU?

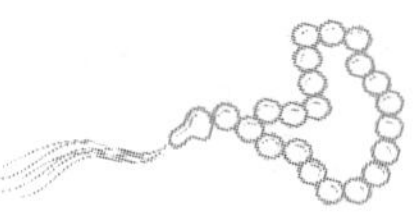

WRITE YOUR DUA, HADITH, OR QUR'AN SELECTION HERE:

WHAT DOES THIS SELECTION MEAN TO YOU?

HOW DOES THIS RELATE TO YOUR DAILY LIFE?

WHAT ARE THREE THINGS THAT YOU CAN EXPRESS SHUKR FOR IN YOUR DUA TODAY? WHY ARE YOU GRATEFUL FOR THEM?

WHAT IS ONE THING THAT YOU WOULD LIKE TO ASK FOR IN YOUR DUA TODAY? HOW WOULD IT HELP YOU IF ALLAH GRANTED IT TO YOU?

Health

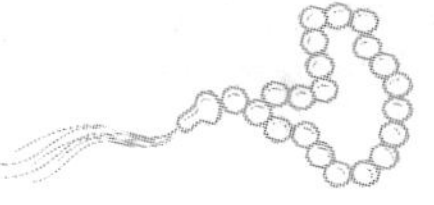

"There are two blessings which many people waste: health and free time."

[Sahih al-Bukhari]

WHAT DOES THIS HADITH MEAN TO YOU?

HOW DOES THIS RELATE TO YOUR DAILY LIFE?

WHAT ARE THREE THINGS THAT YOU CAN EXPRESS SHUKR FOR IN YOUR DUA TODAY? WHY ARE YOU GRATEFUL FOR THEM?

WHAT IS ONE THING THAT YOU WOULD LIKE TO ASK FOR IN YOUR DUA TODAY? HOW WOULD IT HELP YOU IF ALLAH GRANTED IT TO YOU?

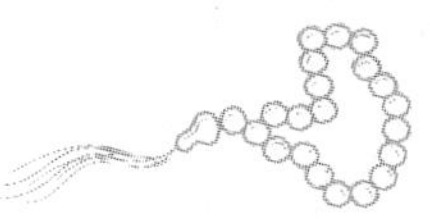

Miqdam bin Madikarib said: “I heard the Messenger of Allah (SAW) say, ‘A human being fills no worse vessel than his stomach. It is sufficient for a human being to eat a few mouthfuls to keep his spine straight. But if he must (fill it), then one third for food, one third for drink, and one third for air.’”

[Sunan Ibn Majah]

WHAT DOES THIS HADITH MEAN TO YOU?

HOW DOES THIS RELATE TO YOUR DAILY LIFE?

WHAT ARE THREE THINGS THAT YOU CAN EXPRESS SHUKR FOR IN YOUR DUA TODAY? WHY ARE YOU GRATEFUL FOR THEM?

WHAT IS ONE THING THAT YOU WOULD LIKE TO ASK FOR IN YOUR DUA TODAY? HOW WOULD IT HELP YOU IF ALLAH GRANTED IT TO YOU?

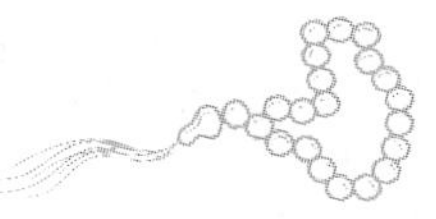

Ibn `Abbas narrated: The Prophet (SAW) said, "Healing is in three things: cupping, a gulp of honey or cauterization (branding with fire), but I forbid my followers to use cauterization (branding with fire)."

[Sahih al-Bukhari]

WHAT DOES THIS HADITH MEAN TO YOU?

HOW DOES THIS RELATE TO YOUR DAILY LIFE?

WHAT ARE THREE THINGS THAT YOU CAN EXPRESS SHUKR FOR IN YOUR DUA TODAY? WHY ARE YOU GRATEFUL FOR THEM?

WHAT IS ONE THING THAT YOU WOULD LIKE TO ASK FOR IN YOUR DUA TODAY? HOW WOULD IT HELP YOU IF ALLAH GRANTED IT TO YOU?

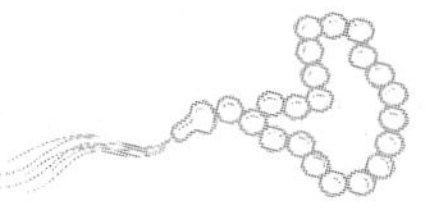

Anas bin Malik narrated: Allah's Messenger (SAW) said, "(Death from) plague is martyrdom for every Muslim."

[Sahih al-Bukhari]

WHAT DOES THIS HADITH MEAN TO YOU?

HOW DOES THIS RELATE TO YOUR DAILY LIFE?

WHAT ARE THREE THINGS THAT YOU CAN EXPRESS SHUKR FOR IN YOUR DUA TODAY? WHY ARE YOU GRATEFUL FOR THEM?

WHAT IS ONE THING THAT YOU WOULD LIKE TO ASK FOR IN YOUR DUA TODAY? HOW WOULD IT HELP YOU IF ALLAH GRANTED IT TO YOU?

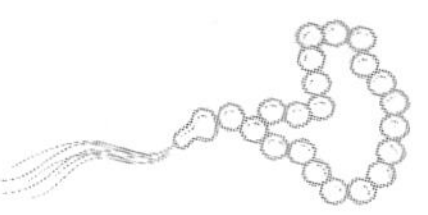

O Allah, I hope for Your mercy. Do not leave me to myself even for the blinking of an eye. Correct all of my affairs for me. There is none worthy of worship but you.

[Abu Dawud]

WHAT DOES THIS DUA MEAN TO YOU?

HOW DOES THIS RELATE TO YOUR DAILY LIFE?

WHAT ARE THREE THINGS THAT YOU CAN EXPRESS SHUKR FOR IN YOUR DUA TODAY? WHY ARE YOU GRATEFUL FOR THEM?

WHAT IS ONE THING THAT YOU WOULD LIKE TO ASK FOR IN YOUR DUA TODAY? HOW WOULD IT HELP YOU IF ALLAH GRANTED IT TO YOU?

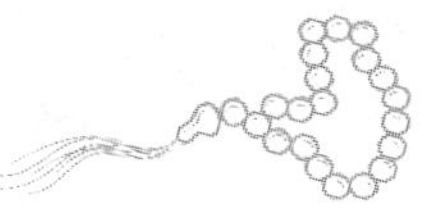

O humanity! Indeed, there has come to you a warning from your Lord, a cure for what is in the hearts, a guide, and a mercy for the believers.

[Qur'an, 10:57]

WHAT DOES THIS AYAH MEAN TO YOU?

HOW DOES THIS RELATE TO YOUR DAILY LIFE?

WHAT ARE THREE THINGS THAT YOU CAN EXPRESS SHUKR FOR IN YOUR DUA TODAY? WHY ARE YOU GRATEFUL FOR THEM?

WHAT IS ONE THING THAT YOU WOULD LIKE TO ASK FOR IN YOUR DUA TODAY? HOW WOULD IT HELP YOU IF ALLAH GRANTED IT TO YOU?

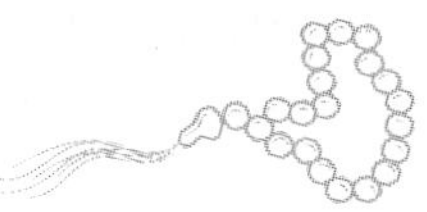

O believers! Seek comfort in patience and prayer.
God is truly with those who are patient.

[Qur'an, 2:153]

WHAT DOES THIS AYAH MEAN TO YOU?

HOW DOES THIS RELATE TO YOUR DAILY LIFE?

WHAT ARE THREE THINGS THAT YOU CAN EXPRESS SHUKR FOR IN YOUR DUA TODAY? WHY ARE YOU GRATEFUL FOR THEM?

WHAT IS ONE THING THAT YOU WOULD LIKE TO ASK FOR IN YOUR DUA TODAY? HOW WOULD IT HELP YOU IF ALLAH GRANTED IT TO YOU?

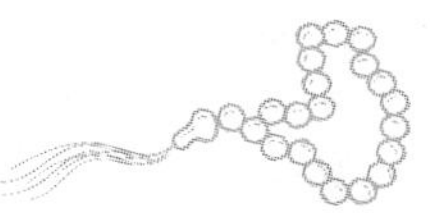

Abu Hurairah (RA) reported: The Messenger of Allah (SAW) said, “Verily, Allah has pardoned my nation for what occurs within themselves, as long as they do not speak of it or act upon it.”

[Sahih Muslim]

WHAT DOES THIS HADITH MEAN TO YOU?

HOW DOES THIS RELATE TO YOUR DAILY LIFE?

WHAT ARE THREE THINGS THAT YOU CAN EXPRESS SHUKR FOR IN YOUR DUA TODAY? WHY ARE YOU GRATEFUL FOR THEM?

WHAT IS ONE THING THAT YOU WOULD LIKE TO ASK FOR IN YOUR DUA TODAY? HOW WOULD IT HELP YOU IF ALLAH GRANTED IT TO YOU?

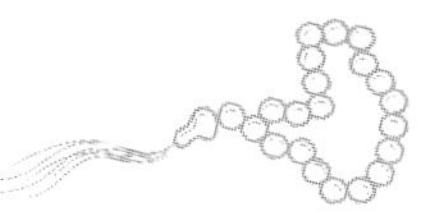

Abu Said Al-Khudri and Abu Hurairah (RA) reported that the Prophet (SAW) said: "Never a believer is stricken with a discomfort, an illness, an anxiety, a grief, or mental worry, or even the pricking of a thorn, but Allah will expiate his sins on account of his patience."

[Al-Bukhari and Muslim]

WHAT DOES THIS HADITH MEAN TO YOU?

HOW DOES THIS RELATE TO YOUR DAILY LIFE?

WHAT ARE THREE THINGS THAT YOU CAN EXPRESS SHUKR FOR IN YOUR DUA TODAY? WHY ARE YOU GRATEFUL FOR THEM?

WHAT IS ONE THING THAT YOU WOULD LIKE TO ASK FOR IN YOUR DUA TODAY? HOW WOULD IT HELP YOU IF ALLAH GRANTED IT TO YOU?

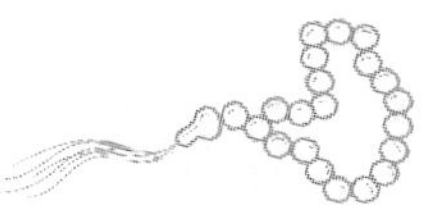

"O Allah, I seek refuge in You from grief and sadness, from weakness and from laziness, from miserliness and from cowardice, from being overcome by debt and overpowered by men [i.e., others]."

[Bukhari]

WHAT DOES THIS DUA MEAN TO YOU?

HOW DOES THIS RELATE TO YOUR DAILY LIFE?

WHAT ARE THREE THINGS THAT YOU CAN EXPRESS SHUKR FOR IN YOUR DUA TODAY? WHY ARE YOU GRATEFUL FOR THEM?

WHAT IS ONE THING THAT YOU WOULD LIKE TO ASK FOR IN YOUR DUA TODAY? HOW WOULD IT HELP YOU IF ALLAH GRANTED IT TO YOU?

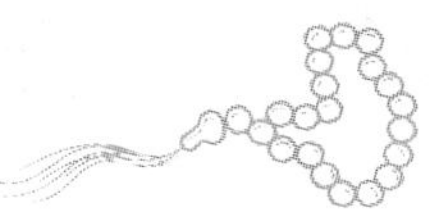

WRITE YOUR DUA, HADITH, OR QUR'AN SELECTION HERE:

WHAT DOES THIS SELECTION MEAN TO YOU?

HOW DOES THIS RELATE TO YOUR DAILY LIFE?

WHAT ARE THREE THINGS THAT YOU CAN EXPRESS SHUKR FOR IN YOUR DUA TODAY? WHY ARE YOU GRATEFUL FOR THEM?

WHAT IS ONE THING THAT YOU WOULD LIKE TO ASK FOR IN YOUR DUA TODAY? HOW WOULD IT HELP YOU IF ALLAH GRANTED IT TO YOU?

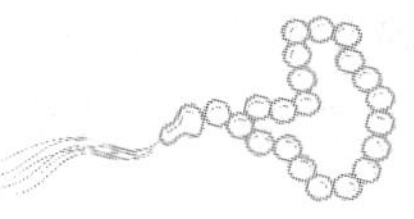

WRITE YOUR DUA, HADITH, OR QUR'AN SELECTION HERE:

WHAT DOES THIS SELECTION MEAN TO YOU?

HOW DOES THIS RELATE TO YOUR DAILY LIFE?

WHAT ARE THREE THINGS THAT YOU CAN EXPRESS SHUKR FOR IN YOUR DUA TODAY? WHY ARE YOU GRATEFUL FOR THEM?

WHAT IS ONE THING THAT YOU WOULD LIKE TO ASK FOR IN YOUR DUA TODAY? HOW WOULD IT HELP YOU IF ALLAH GRANTED IT TO YOU?

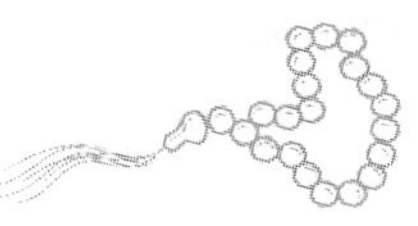

WRITE YOUR DUA, HADITH, OR QUR'AN SELECTION HERE:

WHAT DOES THIS SELECTION MEAN TO YOU?

HOW DOES THIS RELATE TO YOUR DAILY LIFE?

WHAT ARE THREE THINGS THAT YOU CAN EXPRESS SHUKR FOR IN YOUR DUA TODAY? WHY ARE YOU GRATEFUL FOR THEM?

WHAT IS ONE THING THAT YOU WOULD LIKE TO ASK FOR IN YOUR DUA TODAY? HOW WOULD IT HELP YOU IF ALLAH GRANTED IT TO YOU?

Community

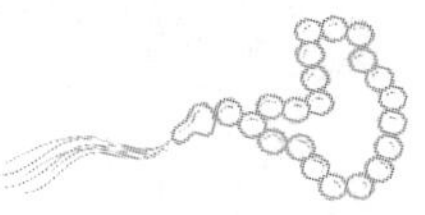

Nu'man bin Bashir (RA) reported: The Messenger of Allah (SAW) said, "The believers in their mutual kindness, compassion, and sympathy are just like one body. When one of the limbs suffers, the whole body responds to it with wakefulness and fever."

[Sahih al-Bukhari]

WHAT DOES THIS HADITH MEAN TO YOU?

HOW DOES THIS RELATE TO YOUR DAILY LIFE?

WHAT ARE THREE THINGS THAT YOU CAN EXPRESS SHUKR FOR IN YOUR DUA TODAY? WHY ARE YOU GRATEFUL FOR THEM?

WHAT IS ONE THING THAT YOU WOULD LIKE TO ASK FOR IN YOUR DUA TODAY? HOW WOULD IT HELP YOU IF ALLAH GRANTED IT TO YOU?

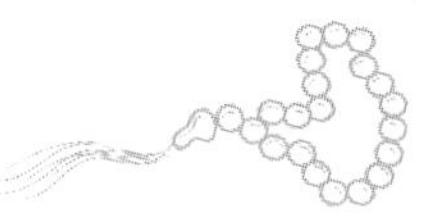

Abu Musa narrated: The Prophet (SAW) said, "A believer to another believer is like a building whose different parts enforce each other." The Prophet (SAW) then clasped his hands with the fingers interlaced (while saying that).

[Sahih al-Bukhari]

WHAT DOES THIS HADITH MEAN TO YOU?

HOW DOES THIS RELATE TO YOUR DAILY LIFE?

WHAT ARE THREE THINGS THAT YOU CAN EXPRESS SHUKR FOR IN YOUR DUA TODAY? WHY ARE YOU GRATEFUL FOR THEM?

WHAT IS ONE THING THAT YOU WOULD LIKE TO ASK FOR IN YOUR DUA TODAY? HOW WOULD IT HELP YOU IF ALLAH GRANTED IT TO YOU?

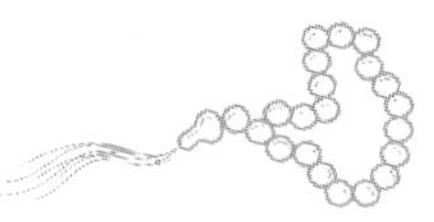

Abu Dharr narrated that the Messenger of Allah (SAW) said: "Your smiling in the face of your brother is charity, commanding good and forbidding evil is charity, your giving directions to a man lost in the land is charity for you. Your seeing for a man with bad sight is a charity for you, your removal of a rock, a thorn, or a bone from the road is charity for you. Your pouring what remains from your bucket into the bucket of your brother is charity for you."

[Jami at-Tirmidhi]

WHAT DOES THIS HADITH MEAN TO YOU?

HOW DOES THIS RELATE TO YOUR DAILY LIFE?

WHAT ARE THREE THINGS THAT YOU CAN EXPRESS SHUKR FOR IN YOUR DUA TODAY? WHY ARE YOU GRATEFUL FOR THEM?

WHAT IS ONE THING THAT YOU WOULD LIKE TO ASK FOR IN YOUR DUA TODAY? HOW WOULD IT HELP YOU IF ALLAH GRANTED IT TO YOU?

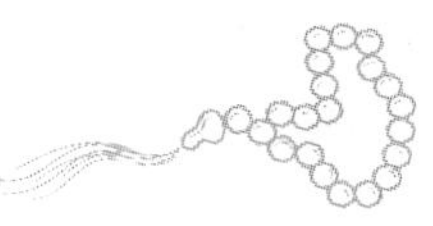

Anas bin Malik narrated: Allah's Messenger (SAW) said, "There is none amongst the Muslims who plants a tree or sows seeds, and then a bird, or a person or an animal eats from it, but is regarded as a charitable gift for him."

[Sahih al-Bukhari]

WHAT DOES THIS HADITH MEAN TO YOU?

HOW DOES THIS RELATE TO YOUR DAILY LIFE?

WHAT ARE THREE THINGS THAT YOU CAN EXPRESS SHUKR FOR IN YOUR DUA TODAY? WHY ARE YOU GRATEFUL FOR THEM?

WHAT IS ONE THING THAT YOU WOULD LIKE TO ASK FOR IN YOUR DUA TODAY? HOW WOULD IT HELP YOU IF ALLAH GRANTED IT TO YOU?

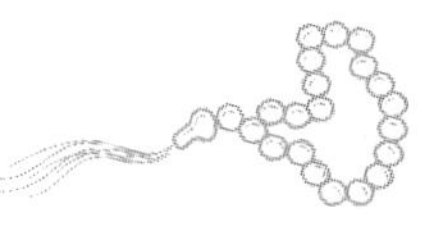

And what is it with you? You do not fight in the cause of God and for oppressed men, women, and children who cry out, "Our Lord! Deliver us from this land of oppressors! Appoint for us a savior; appoint for us a helper—all by Your grace."

[Qur'an, 4:75]

WHAT DOES THIS AYAH MEAN TO YOU?

HOW DOES THIS RELATE TO YOUR DAILY LIFE?

WHAT ARE THREE THINGS THAT YOU CAN EXPRESS SHUKR FOR IN YOUR DUA TODAY? WHY ARE YOU GRATEFUL FOR THEM?

WHAT IS ONE THING THAT YOU WOULD LIKE TO ASK FOR IN YOUR DUA TODAY? HOW WOULD IT HELP YOU IF ALLAH GRANTED IT TO YOU?

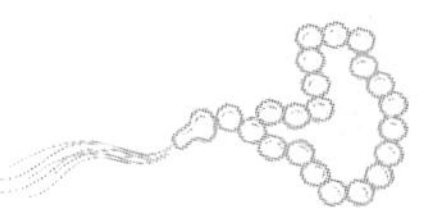

And those who come after them will pray, "Our Lord! Forgive us and our fellow believers who preceded us in faith, and do not allow bitterness into our hearts toward those who believe. Our Lord! Indeed, You are Ever Gracious, Most Merciful."

[Qur'an, 59:10]

WHAT DOES THIS DUA MEAN TO YOU?

HOW DOES THIS RELATE TO YOUR DAILY LIFE?

WHAT ARE THREE THINGS THAT YOU CAN EXPRESS SHUKR FOR IN YOUR DUA TODAY? WHY ARE YOU GRATEFUL FOR THEM?

WHAT IS ONE THING THAT YOU WOULD LIKE TO ASK FOR IN YOUR DUA TODAY? HOW WOULD IT HELP YOU IF ALLAH GRANTED IT TO YOU?

O Allah, feed the one who has fed me and [provide] drink to the one who has given me a drink.

[Muslim]

WHAT DOES THIS DUA MEAN TO YOU?

HOW DOES THIS RELATE TO YOUR DAILY LIFE?

WHAT ARE THREE THINGS THAT YOU CAN EXPRESS SHUKR FOR IN YOUR DUA TODAY? WHY ARE YOU GRATEFUL FOR THEM?

WHAT IS ONE THING THAT YOU WOULD LIKE TO ASK FOR IN YOUR DUA TODAY? HOW WOULD IT HELP YOU IF ALLAH GRANTED IT TO YOU?

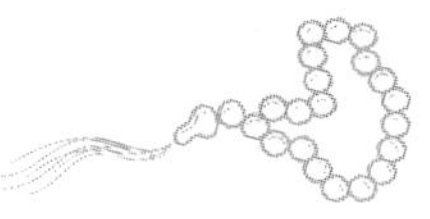

Those who spend their wealth in the cause of God and do not follow their charity with reminders of their generosity or hurtful words—they will get their reward from their Lord. . . . Kind words and forgiveness are better than charity followed by injury.

[Qur'an, 2:262]

WHAT DOES THIS AYAH MEAN TO YOU?

HOW DOES THIS RELATE TO YOUR DAILY LIFE?

WHAT ARE THREE THINGS THAT YOU CAN EXPRESS SHUKR FOR IN YOUR DUA TODAY? WHY ARE YOU GRATEFUL FOR THEM?

WHAT IS ONE THING THAT YOU WOULD LIKE TO ASK FOR IN YOUR DUA TODAY? HOW WOULD IT HELP YOU IF ALLAH GRANTED IT TO YOU?

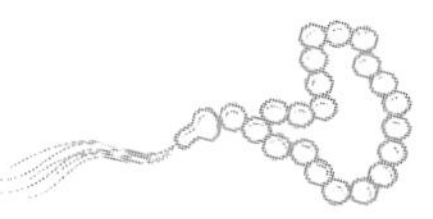

And so We have made you believers an upright community so that you may be witnesses over humanity and that the Messenger may be a witness over you.

[Qur'an, 2:143]

WHAT DOES THIS AYAH MEAN TO YOU?

HOW DOES THIS RELATE TO YOUR DAILY LIFE?

WHAT ARE THREE THINGS THAT YOU CAN EXPRESS SHUKR FOR IN YOUR DUA TODAY? WHY ARE YOU GRATEFUL FOR THEM?

WHAT IS ONE THING THAT YOU WOULD LIKE TO ASK FOR IN YOUR DUA TODAY? HOW WOULD IT HELP YOU IF ALLAH GRANTED IT TO YOU?

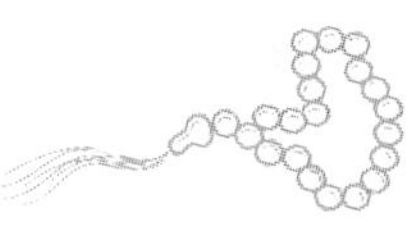

WRITE YOUR DUA, HADITH, OR QUR'AN SELECTION HERE:

WHAT DOES THIS SELECTION MEAN TO YOU?

HOW DOES THIS RELATE TO YOUR DAILY LIFE?

WHAT ARE THREE THINGS THAT YOU CAN EXPRESS SHUKR FOR IN YOUR DUA TODAY? WHY ARE YOU GRATEFUL FOR THEM?

WHAT IS ONE THING THAT YOU WOULD LIKE TO ASK FOR IN YOUR DUA TODAY? HOW WOULD IT HELP YOU IF ALLAH GRANTED IT TO YOU?

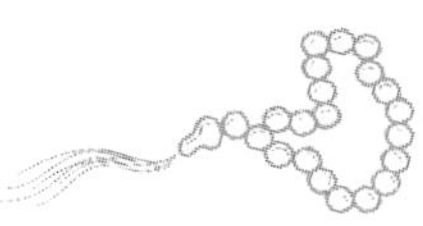

WRITE YOUR DUA, HADITH, OR QUR'AN SELECTION HERE:

WHAT DOES THIS SELECTION MEAN TO YOU?

HOW DOES THIS RELATE TO YOUR DAILY LIFE?

WHAT ARE THREE THINGS THAT YOU CAN EXPRESS SHUKR FOR IN YOUR DUA TODAY? WHY ARE YOU GRATEFUL FOR THEM?

WHAT IS ONE THING THAT YOU WOULD LIKE TO ASK FOR IN YOUR DUA TODAY? HOW WOULD IT HELP YOU IF ALLAH GRANTED IT TO YOU?

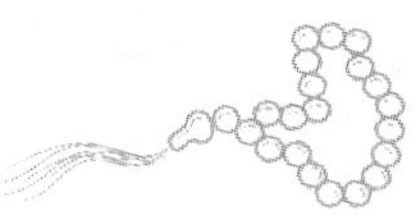

WRITE YOUR DUA, HADITH, OR QUR'AN SELECTION HERE:

WHAT DOES THIS SELECTION MEAN TO YOU?

HOW DOES THIS RELATE TO YOUR DAILY LIFE?

WHAT ARE THREE THINGS THAT YOU CAN EXPRESS SHUKR FOR IN YOUR DUA TODAY? WHY ARE YOU GRATEFUL FOR THEM?

WHAT IS ONE THING THAT YOU WOULD LIKE TO ASK FOR IN YOUR DUA TODAY? HOW WOULD IT HELP YOU IF ALLAH GRANTED IT TO YOU?

Reflections

WHAT ARE YOUR BIGGEST TAKEAWAYS FROM THE EXPERIENCE OF COMPLETING THIS JOURNAL?

HAVE YOU NOTICED SPIRITUAL GROWTH SINCE THE BEGINNING OF YOUR JOURNALING EXPERIENCE? EXPLAIN THE CHANGES YOU'VE RECOGNIZED AND HOW THEY HAVE AFFECTED YOUR LIFE.

WHAT HAVE YOU LEARNED ABOUT YOURSELF DURING YOUR JOURNALING EXPERIENCE?

AS YOU MOVE FORWARD IN YOUR SPIRITUAL JOURNEY, WHAT WOULD YOU LIKE TO TAKE FORWARD FROM THIS EXPERIENCE?

Acknowledgments

I would first like to express my gratitude to Allah (SWT) for the talent with which He has blessed me, as well as the opportunities to use this talent for His sake and in the service of others.

A very heartfelt thank you to Ulysses Press for coming up with the idea of a journaling experience that caters to Muslim women, one of the most overlooked demographics, in my opinion. To Casie Vogel and the Ulysses Press team behind this book, thank you for your support, guidance, and feedback throughout this process and for fostering a collaborative relationship from the very beginning.

To Hafsa Khan (@hafandhaf), for agreeing to be a part of this project and for your cover art that so beautifully brought together the many ideas we threw at you.

To Shaykh Ibad Wali, for lending your expertise and guidance.

To Nafeiza Khan, for being my sounding board for almost everything I write, including this journal, supporting me in my dreams of pursuing this profession, and giving birth to me.

To Nasheela Khan, for bringing me to Sister Hamida's class that first day and answering the many calls I made to pick your brain for this journal.

To Zayna Deonath, for indulging me with that first 4 a.m. brainstorm session that set this book in motion.

And to Sadiqur Rahman, for helping me decide on a title for this journal and your words of encouragement all the way through.

About the Author

Gabrielle Deonath is a Guyanese American Muslim writer and editor. First published at age sixteen, she penned personal essays on her experiences navigating the world as a Muslim teenager for VirtualMosque.com and *SISTERS Magazine*. For five years, she served as an assistant editor at *Brown Girl Magazine* and is one of the editors of the magazine's first-ever print anthology, *untold: defining moments of the uprooted*. She earned a bachelor's degree in communications from Adelphi University in 2018 and went on to work for mission-based organizations, including Global Citizen and Girl Scouts of the USA. Gabrielle hopes to continue to give a voice to those without a platform and provide authentic representation of minorities and marginalized communities through storytelling. She lives in New York City, at the bustling intersection of her passion for the written word and her deep love for her faith.